DINOSAURS
BIG AND SMALL
by Michael Teitelbaum

THE FACTS ABOUT DINOSAURS

The Rourke Corporation, Inc.
Vero Beach, FL 32964

© 1994 The Rourke Corporation, Inc.

Library of Congress Cataloging-in-Publication Data
Teitelbaum, Michael.
      Dinosaurs, big and small / by Michael Teitelbaum.
          p.   cm. — (The Facts about dinosaurs)
      ISBN 0-86593-352-9
      1. Dinosaurs—Juvenile literature. [1. Dinosaurs.] I. Title. II. Series.
QE862.D5T425   1994
567.9'1—dc20   93-50058
                                                                        CIP
Printed in the USA   AC

CONTENTS

ALBERTOSAURUS
(al-BER-tuh-sawr-us)

Albertosaurus was a large, **carrion**-eating dinosaur. The huge Albertosaurus walked in a side-to-side fashion and moved very slowly. It was difficult for Albertosaurus to hunt **prey**. This is why it feasted on the remains of other hunters' kills.

Albertosaurus had a large head and powerful jaws, like its relative, Tyrannosaurus Rex. But Albertosaurus had more teeth than Tyrannosaurus Rex. Albertosaurus grew to 26 feet in length and weighed up to two tons.

Albertosaurus got its name because its first **fossil** was found in Alberta, Canada. Other Albertosaurus fossils have been found in the western United States and Mongolia.

Albertosaurus's arms were so tiny that the giant dinosaur probably never used them at all.

CORYTHOSAURUS
(ko-RITH-uh-sawr-us)

Corythosaurus means "helmet lizard." It belonged to a group of plant-eating dinosaurs called **Hadrosaurs**. They were also known as duck-billed dinosaurs, because they had long flat bills, like ducks. Unlike ducks, however, Hadrosaurs had teeth and spent most of their time in forests, not in water.

Corythosaurus had a large, flat crest that ran down the middle of its head. The crest was hollow, narrow, and shaped like a dinner plate. Females and young Corythosaurus had smaller crests than males.

Its heavy tail was used for balance while it stood on its back legs and slowly ate the leaves off trees. Its teeth were packed together tightly and were perfect for munching on tough forest greenery.

Corythosaurus had strong family instincts. It lived in a colony so that some members could watch the young while others gathered food.

DEINOSUCHUS
(dye-no-SUE-kus)

Deinosuchus looked like a giant crocodile. It belonged to a group related to dinosaurs called **Crocodilians**. Like the modern crocodile, this **amphibian** split its time between the water and the land, spending most of its time in jungle rivers. It had a long snout filled with sharp teeth.

Deinosuchus ate fish and small land creatures. It would hide underwater, with just its eyes above the surface, waiting for its next meal.

Deinosuchus had tough armor on its back. When it got into a fight, usually with another Crocodilian, it would use its powerful tail to try and flip its opponent over to expose its throat and belly. These were the areas where Deinosuchus was vulnerable to attack.

Despite its great size, Deinosuchus needed very little food to survive.

VELOCIRAPTOR
(veh-loss-ih-RAP-tor)

This speedy hunter had three fingers on each hand. Each finger had a sharp claw on it. The claw was used to slash Velociraptor's victims. Its hands were also able to grasp and hold tightly.

Velociraptor had sharp claws on its feet. It would grab its victims with its hands. This would keep its enemies at arm's length, while it delivered slashing kicks.

Velociraptor was not afraid to pick on dinosaurs much bigger than itself. This six-foot-tall dinosaur weighed only a few hundred pounds. But one of its skeletons was found clutching the head of a **Protoceratops**. Protoceratops could weigh as much as two tons—that's 4,000 pounds!

*The smaller Velociraptor was more intelligent than the large **Carnosaurs** like Tyrannosaurus Rex.*

10

PARASAUROLOPHUS
(par-ah-sawr-OL-uh-fus)

Parasaurolophus was one of the largest members of the plant-eating family of dinosaurs called Hadrosaurs. It was 33 feet long, and weighed up to four tons.

This duck-billed dinosaur had a very special crest on its head. It was a curved, hollow horn that was attached to the front of the head and swept backwards.

This horn was more than six feet long. Inside the horn, two tubes went up to the top, and two tubes ran back down. The tubes going up into the crest were attached to the Parasaurolophus's nostrils. The tubes that went down were breathing tubes, and they went into its lungs.

Parasaurolophus made a loud bellowing sound to scare off enemies by snorting through its long breathing tubes.

STRUTHIOMIMUS
(strooth-ee-uh-MY-mus)

This toothless egg-stealer was one of the fastest and one of the smartest dinosaurs that ever lived. It looked like a large bird, with a short body, a long tail, and a curved neck. Its head was small, but its eyes were very large.

Struthiomimus had long, finger-like claws that could easily pull fruit from palm and fig trees. This dinosaur "thief" got its favorite meal by stealing the eggs of other dinosaurs. It used its strong claws to tear open the eggs.

When **paleontologists** found its skeleton they thought it resembled an ostrich. The name Struthiomimus means "ostrich mimic." Struthiomimus is a member of the **Ornithomimus** family of dinosaurs. Ornithomimus means "hollow-tail lizards."

Struthiomimus was one of the fastest land animals that ever lived, running at speeds up to 50 miles per hour.

14

BRACHIOSAURUS
(BRAK-ee-uh-sawr-us)

Brachiosaurus was the largest of all known dinosaurs. This plant-eater could reach a length of 90 feet and a weight of 100 tons. It had a very long neck, like a giraffe. This let the dinosaur **browse** in the leafy branches at the tops of trees. When it stretched its neck it could reach a height of 40 feet.

Most dinosaurs had their longest legs in the back. Brachiosaurus had its longest legs in the front. It had a short tail and a strong back. Its head was small and its teeth were tiny.

Because of its huge size and the nostrils on the top of its head, scientists used to think it lived in the water. Now they believe that Brachiosaurus lived on land.

Brachiosaurus weighed as much as 20 large elephants.

16

TYRANNOSAURUS REX
(tye-RAN-uh-sawr-us rex)

Tyrannosaurus Rex was a large, meat-eater. It was the most deadly killing machine that ever lived. Its skull was very large and sometimes looked as if it was too big for its body. The skull was so big to make room for Tyrannosaurus Rex's long sharp teeth.

Paleontologists have dug up many Tyrannosaurus Rex fossils. They discovered that, in a number of cases, the huge dinosaur's backbone was welded together. Tyrannosaurus Rex would use its big head to smash into its prey. This would stun its victim, making for an easier kill.

The shocks from smashing its head caused the "tyrant lizard" to suffer terrible pain.

Even a giant dinosaur like Albertosaurus feared a battle with mighty Tyrannosaurus Rex.

18

PTERANODON
(ter-ANN-uh-don)

Pteranodon was not actually a dinosaur. It was part of a family of flying reptiles called **Pterosaurs**. This winged and toothless fish-eater weighed about 33 pounds. Its body was the size of a turkey.

It had a long bony **crest** on the top of its head. Although no one is sure, paleontologists believe that this crest may have been used as a brake for landing, or as a rudder for steering during flight, since Pteranodon had no tail. The crest simply may have been there to balance against Pteranodon's huge beak.

Pteranodon was more of a glider than a true flyer. Because of this, it could only fly in a light or moderate wind.

Pteranodon's wingspan was 27 feet—the size of a small airplane.

DILOPHOSAURUS
(dye-LO-fuh-sawr-us)

In 1954 the very first Dilophosaurus fossils were found in Arizona by a Navajo Indian. These fossils were found in rocks from the early **Jurassic** Period.

With these remains, scientists have been able to reconstruct the appearance of Dilophosaurus. It was about 20 feet long, making it one of the biggest dinosaurs of its time. Dilophosaurus was a meat-eating dinosaur. Its strong body and sharp teeth made Dilophosaurus a predator to fear.

Dilophosaurus belonged to a family of dinosaurs called the Megalosaurids, which means "great lizards." Megalosaurids lived over many millions of years and several different species of dinosaurs evolved from Dilophosaurus.

A male Dilophosaurus had a paper-thin crest on his head which he used as a display to frighten enemies away from his food.

22

GLOSSARY

Amphibian—An animal that lives both on land and in the water.

Browse—To feed. Usually used to refer to the eating habits of plant-eaters.

Carnosaurs—Large, slow-moving, meat-eating dinosaurs. They had huge heads and teeth and were the kings of the dinosaur world.

Carrion—The flesh of an already dead animal. A dinosaur that eats carrion is eating the meat of someone else's kill.

Crest—A crown-like piece of bone that stuck out of the back of the head of some dinosaurs.

Crocodilian—A family of prehistoric amphibious reptiles that greatly resembled modern-day crocodiles.

Fossils—The petrified bones of ancient animals like dinosaurs.

Hadrosaurs—Duck-billed dinosaurs.

Jurassic—The dinosaur age beginning 190 million years ago and ending 135 million years ago.

Ornithomimus—A family of fast, intelligent meat-eaters known as "hollow-tail lizards."

Paleontologist—A scientist who studies dinosaurs.

Prey—The victim of a meat-eating animal.

Protoceratops—One of the smaller horned dinosaurs. This plant-eater grew to six feet long and weighed up to two tons.

Pterosaurs—Flying reptiles that lived at the same time as the dinosaurs.